I0171241

# SPIRITUAL BLESSING

Stephen Kaung

Copyright © 2015
Christian Testimony Ministry
Richmond, Virginia
All Rights Reserved

ISBN: 978-1-942521-17-4

Available from:

Christian Testimony Ministry
4424 Huguenot Road
Richmond, Virginia 23235

www.christiantestimonyministry.com

Printed in USA

# CONTENTS

Unless otherwise indicated,
Scripture quotations are from
The American Standard Version 1901

# SPIRITUAL BLESSING DEFINED

*Ephesians 1:3-14—Blessed be the God and Father of our Lord Jesus Christ, who has blessed us with every spiritual blessing in the heavenlies in Christ; according as he has chosen us in him before the world's foundation, that we should be holy and blameless before him in love; having marked us out beforehand for [sonship] through Jesus Christ to himself; according to the good pleasure of his will, to the praise of the glory of his grace, wherein he has taken us into favour in the Beloved: in whom we have redemption through his blood, the forgiveness of offences, according to the riches of his grace; which he has caused to abound towards us in all wisdom and intelligence, having made known to us the mystery of his will, according to his good pleasure which he purposed in himself for the administration of the fulness of times; to head up all things in the Christ, the things in the heavens and the things upon the earth; in him, in whom we have also obtained an inheritance, being marked out beforehand according to the purpose of him who works all things according to the counsel of his own will, that we should be to the praise of his glory who have pre-trusted in the Christ: in whom ye also have trusted, having heard the word of the truth, the glad tidings of your salvation; in whom also, having believed, ye have been sealed with the Holy Spirit of promise, who is the earnest of our inheritance to the redemption of the acquired possession to the praise of his glory.*

Shall we pray:

*Dear Lord, we want to thank Thee for gathering us together, and we are gathered unto Thy name. We believe that Thou art here with us, and we want to remove our shoes, prostrate ourselves before Thee, and say, "Lord, what hast Thou to say to us? Speak, Thy servants heareth." We ask in the name of our Lord Jesus. Amen.*

Our God is the God of blessing. He is love; therefore He desires to bless. He is the fountain of all blessings; all blessings flow from Him. In the very beginning when God created man, after He made man in His own image according to His own likeness, then He blessed them (see Genesis 1:26-28). It is the desire of our God to bless. He blessed them that they may be fruitful, fill the earth, subdue the enemy, and bring everything back to the feet of God. After God created the world in six days, on the seventh day He rested and He blessed that day. So after man was created, immediately he was introduced into God's rest. This is our God.

God wants to bless. He does not want to curse. Curse came in after the fall of man. In Genesis 3, after man sinned, then curse came into this world, because our God is a righteous God, and will not the Judge of man be righteous? Because of the fall of man, curse came upon this earth. Curse came upon the enemy of God, upon man, and upon woman. But again, we see it is not the desire of God to curse; His desire is to bless. I think this is very evident if we look at the story of Job.

## THE BLESSING OF GOD UPON JOB

Job feared God and abstained from evil. He was a perfect man and God used Job to challenge His enemy. But His enemy said to God: "Is there not a reason for Job to fear You? It is because You have blessed him. You have put a hedge around him. You blessed his family, You blessed all of his works, and that is why Job fears You. If You take away the things that You have blessed him with, see if he will curse You to Your face."

Curse is the desire of the enemy of God. He has no desire to bless anyone. His desire is to curse because that is what he is. God took up his challenge and said, "Okay, you can touch everything that he has but do not touch him." So Satan went out and destroyed all his children, all his property, and Job bowed down and said, "God gave and God has taken away; blessed be the name of the Lord" (Job 1:21b).

Another day Satan appeared before God and God again challenged him: "Did you notice my servant Job? Even after you attacked him and took away all that he was blessed with, he sinned not." The enemy was so subtle, so wicked, he said, "A man will gladly give up everything to keep his life. If you touch his body, then You will see what happens." God said, "He is in thy hand; only spare his life." So Satan attacked him with boils all over his body. He sat in ashes, scratching himself. Even his wife suggested, "Curse God and die." But Job said, "We have received good from God, shall we not receive evil from Him too?" (see Job 2:10). He did not sin with his lips.

God allowed Satan to attack Job. Why? It is because God wanted to bless him even more. There was something in Job that gave the enemy the ground—his own self-righteousness. And God made use of Satan to purify Job of his self-righteousness in order that He might bless him even more. At the end of the book of Job, God blessed him with double blessing. It is the blessing of the first-born. So we find that our God loves to bless and He is very reluctant to curse. This is our God.

## TYPES AND SHADOWS

Throughout the Old Testament, you will find that God always wants to bless. After the flood, he blessed Noah and his family. After the tower of Babel, He blessed Abraham. The glory of God appeared to Abraham in Ur of Chaldea. He called him out of the land and from among his kindred to go to the place where God would settle him. By faith, Abraham went out not knowing where he was going; but he knew the God that was leading him. At that time God blessed him, making him a great nation, a great name, a seed, a land, a blessing. And Abraham went out by faith. God promised him the land, but he was a stranger and sojourner in the promised land. God promised him a seed. He said his descendants would be as the stars of the heaven and the sands of the seashore. But until he was a hundred years old, he got only one son. Even though God promised him the land, a physical land, the land of Canaan, yet Abraham knew God and by faith he looked through that physical blessing of the land into the city with foundations whose builder is God (see Hebrews 11:10). God promised him a seed, but it was not Isaac; it is Christ. That is why you find Abraham, by faith, could penetrate through the times, and in John 8:56 it says he saw the day of Christ and he rejoiced. Even though God's promise to

Abraham was earthly, was physical, that was only at the surface. Abraham, by faith, could look into the very depths of God's heart and he could see all the spiritual blessings that God had promised to him.

Through Moses God covenanted with His children, the children of Israel. God gave them the law. We will not appreciate God, we will not appreciate the grace of God until we know ourselves. Because the children of Israel did not know themselves, they could not appreciate the grace of God. So God put them under law, under probation, that they might be shut up to faith to Christ Jesus. You remember how God brought them to Mount Sinai and there gave them the Ten Commandments, the statutes and the ordinances, and made them His people. But under the law the blessing was conditional. If they kept the law, they would be blessed. If they violated the law, they would be cursed. All the promises that God had promised to the children of Israel through Moses were physical, earthly, not spiritual, not heavenly. These are but types and shadows.

At the end of the Old Testament, the last word in Malachi 4:6 is the word *curse*. If it depends upon us, upon our work, it will end up in curse. But thank God, what we find in the Old Testament are but types and shadows; and these things existed until our Lord Jesus came. When our Lord Jesus came, the shadows passed away and the reality set in—changing from the physical to the spiritual, from the earthly to the heavenly, from the temporal to the eternal. So when you come to the New Testament time, you see that God has blessed us with every spiritual blessing in the heavenlies in Christ Jesus. Today, what are we looking for from God? Are we looking to God for physical blessings, earthly blessings, or are we looking to God for that which is spiritual and heavenly?

## SEEKING SPIRITUAL BLESSINGS

Today, even among God's people, consciously or unconsciously, what we are looking for from God is mainly physical blessing. We are looking for blessings on this earth. We think that this is blessing. We do not look at spiritual blessing as *the* blessing but rather at physical blessing as the one we need. That is why today in Christianity the prosperity gospel is so much welcomed by God's people. We want to be blessed physically on earth. We think that is great. That makes us great Christians, having a great God. But the history of the children of Israel ought to teach us a lesson. God promised to bless them with all the physical blessings that you can expect, but were they worthy to enjoy these blessings? If you look into their history, you will find they were blessed but for a very short time. They spent more time under the curse of God than under the blessing of God. Why? It is because when God blessed them and they became fat, then their hearts hardened against God. They rebelled against God and curse came upon them. In other words, they did not deserve to be blessed. They did not know how to enjoy God's blessing. They were unworthy of God's blessing, unfit for it.

In Deuteronomy, chapters 27-28, Moses told the children of Israel before they entered into the promised land: "After you enter in write the law of God on Mount Ebal. There the children of Israel will be divided into two groups. One group will stand on Mount Ebal and the other group will stand on Mount Gerizim. Those who stand on Mount Gerizim will bless and those who stand on Ebal will curse." Then, in Deuteronomy 27, you find it begins with curses, not with blessings. There were twelve curses followed with four blessings in chapter 28; and then, after the blessings there were four more curses. In other words, if God should bless us with physical blessings, what will happen? We will turn away from God; we will fall into curse instead of blessing because we are not worthy.

Does it mean that for believers today there will be no physical blessings whatsoever; that everything is spiritual? No. "Seek ye first the kingdom of God and His righteousness and all these things shall be added unto you (see Matthew 6:33). It is sad to see that God's people today are seeking for physical blessings: "What shall I eat? What shall I drink? What shall I be clothed with?" These are the things that occupy our attention. We look to God our heavenly Father to give us such an abundance of food that we grow fat, and to give us luxuries to enjoy. We are not contented. But godliness with contentment is great gain. We want more: "Bless me, bless me." We consider those who are physically blessed to be blessed. Those who are not physically blessed, we think are not blessed. But look at their lives. How many of those who are only physically blessed truly grow in the Lord, love the Lord with all their hearts, are willing to deny themselves and follow the Lord? Probably most of them are so indulged, so drowned in the physical blessing that they have no time for the Lord or for themselves. What a pity!

Every perfect gift and good gift comes from the Father of light. But remember, God wants to bless His people with real blessing and it is spiritual not physical because God is Spirit. Therefore, He wants to give the best to His people and the best blessing is spiritual blessing. Thank God, He does bless us physically, but remember that it is only within the context of spiritual blessing. In other words, if you are blessed physically first without knowing His spiritual blessing, it will eventually become a curse to your life. But if you seek for spiritual blessing first, with that spiritual blessing, God can bless you physically, and you will be blessed continually. I do hope that we may see this, that this will sink deeply into our hearts. Seek not the world, but seek ye first the kingdom of God and His righteousness and all these things shall be added unto you. Added, not to make you forget God, but added because He is your heavenly Father and He knows all your needs.

In the Old Testament time, the children of Israel were God's earthly people, and you find God's blessings to them were earthly> But we who are the Lord's are a heavenly people; therefore, God's blessing to us is basically spiritual and physical blessings are just added in. So, what should we look for today? Christ has already come. He has already accomplished everything. Therefore, what we should look for is spiritual blessing. Do not look for physical blessings. They are not the best; they are temporal.

The temptation of the enemy today is to draw our attention away from that which is spiritual into that which is physical. That was the temptation he tempted our Lord with while He was on earth: "Turn the stone into bread to fill your stomach. Worship Satan to get the whole world. Jump from the temple that everybody may see You are special. You do not need the cross. You can get the crown."

Dear brothers and sisters, that is the temptation of the enemy, and how he has tempted God's people today. If we are truthful to ourselves, can we honestly say that what we are seeking today is spiritual blessing and not physical blessing? When you say, "God bless me," what do you mean? Let us examine ourselves before the Lord to see what our heart is really seeking after.

Do you know why God's people today do not grow as they should? Why is it that the promised blessing of God, the spiritual blessing of God does not seem to be our portion every day? Why is it that the church today is so poor spiritually? Why is it that our fellowship is like squeezing water out instead of flowing as rivers of living water? Is it because in our daily lives we are occupied more with seeking physical blessings than spiritual blessing? Oh, I do pray that the Lord will change our heart attitude.

Again I say, it does not mean that God will not bless you with physical blessings. If He wills, He will. But if He does not, do not murmur because it may be that without the physical blessings you have more spiritual blessings.

## THE GOD AND FATHER OF OUR LORD JESUS CHRIST

In Ephesians 1:3 it says, "Blessed be the God and Father of our Lord Jesus Christ who has blessed us with every spiritual blessing in the heavenlies in Christ Jesus." In other words, God, who is the God of blessing, now blesses us as the God and Father of our Lord Jesus Christ. After our Lord Jesus rose from the dead, He sent a message to His disciples through Mary: "Go and tell My brethren, I ascend to My Father, your Father, My God, and your God." This is something wonderful! Our Lord Jesus fully shared His Father with us and He fully shared His God with us. God is the God of our Lord Jesus. What a God He is! He is the Father of our Lord Jesus. What a Father He is! And yet because of the redemptive work of our Lord Jesus, the Lord said, "My Father is your Father; My God is your God." The Father that our Lord Jesus knows is to be known by us as well. What a knowledge of the Father!

You know, I often pray, "Lord, I want to know You." Brothers and sisters, how much of God do you really know? How much of God as Father do you really know? The Lord shared His God and His Father with us. He wants us to know God and Father as He knows Him, and it is in that relationship—God as the Father and God of our Lord Jesus—that He has blessed us, not just as the God of creation. Today, we are in a position so much better than the people under the old covenant. Today, God is our God and the God of our Lord Jesus is our God. God is our Father and He is the Father of our Lord Jesus. And it is in that relationship that God has blessed us. So how much more blessing we are being blessed with today!

## GOD HAS BLESSED US

The Bible says, "He *has* blessed us." Now, to us who are in this mortal body, we are still restricted by time and space. So with us, we have the past, present, and future, but with God it is only present. Therefore he said, "He has blessed us." God has already blessed us. We may not have received it yet, experienced it yet, but He has already given. God *has* blessed us. It is not something that is going to happen, but it is something already there because it is in Christ Jesus. It is already there, and all we need to do is experience it more and more by the Spirit of God. God has blessed us with every spiritual blessing. There is not one spiritual blessing that is not there. Why? Because God loves His Son and He has blessed His Son with everything.

It is just like Abraham. He loved Isaac and gave his all to Isaac. God loves His only beloved Son and He gave everything to His Son. God has blessed His Son with every spiritual blessing that He can bless. It is all in Christ Jesus. All the fulness of the Godhead dwells in Him bodily and ye are complete in Him. God, who spared not His Son, will not withhold any good thing from us. He has blessed us with *every* spiritual blessing. So every spiritual blessing that you can think of is already there. It is already given; it is in Christ Jesus, given to you. And all we need to do is to enter in and enjoy it. All the spiritual blessings, all that we need spiritually is already there in the heavenlies.

## IN THE HEAVENLIES

Now we know that the heavenlies or the heavenly places cannot be confined to a physical location. The heavenlies is a heavenly realm. There is a heavenly realm, just like there is an earthly realm. In Ephesians 1 it says that after our Lord Jesus was risen from the dead, God has set Him at His right hand in the heavenlies and made Him Head over all things. He put everything under His feet. That is the heavenlies. Christ Jesus today is sitting at the right hand of God in the heavenlies.

Then in Ephesians 2 it says we are quickened with Him, with Christ. We are risen from the dead with Christ and we are now seated with Christ in the heavenlies. So far as our physical bodies are concerned, we are here, we are sitting here; but spiritually speaking, where are you seated now? You are seated with Christ in the heavenlies, in that heavenly realm.

In that heavenly realm, the angels are there. In Ephesians 3, you find that the principalities and authorities in the heavenlies will learn from the church the all-various wisdom of God. You know, the church has something to teach the angels and they are in the heavenlies. They are ministers to the redeemed of the Lord.

In Ephesians 6 you find the wicked spirits are also in the heavenlies trying to obstruct the will of God. But thank God, in Christ Jesus the church is like a warrior that can stand, withstand, and stand for the will of God. If you take the picture of Canaan, probably it will help you to see it. When the children of Israel entered into Canaan, it was a land flowing with milk and honey. It speaks of the fulness of Christ. God has blessed us with every spiritual blessing in the heavenlies, in Canaan. Everything was there— houses already built, wells already dug, fields already planted. Everything was ready. In Christ Jesus every spiritual blessing is already there. But the children of Israel had to fight the good fight in order to possess their possession because the enemy was also there trying to withstand, to prevent them from enjoying what

God had given to them. It is the same with us today. We have to fight the good fight; but, if we are clothed with Christ, the victory is already there.

## ABIDING IN CHRIST

Where can we enjoy every spiritual blessing? Or to put it in another way: why is it that today we do not enjoy the spiritual blessings that God has promised us? It is because we are not in the heavenlies, experientially speaking. We are too earthly. Our whole attention is focused on the earth. Seek not the things of this world, but seek the things that are above, where our Lord Jesus is, where our life is hid with Christ in God. So if we are more heavenly, if we live in the heavenlies, then we will be able to enjoy all the spiritual blessings that God has promised us in the heavenlies in Christ. Everything is in Christ and God has put us in Christ, but do we abide in Christ? The Lord said, "I am the true vine; ye are the branches. I in you, you in Me." But in order to enjoy the sap, the nourishment of the vine, the branch has to abide in the vine. If we abide in Christ, then He abides in us and all that He is

19

becomes ours. Our problem is not with position because position has nothing to do with us. Position is what God has done in Christ Jesus for us. It is finished. So if we believe in the Lord Jesus, that position is already there. We are in Christ. But our problem is with our condition. Are we abiding in Christ Jesus? How?

In I John 2 we are told that there is an anointing within us. The Holy Spirit dwells in us. He will teach us in all things, great and small, and what He teaches is true and is not false. If we obey the teaching of the anointing, we abide in Christ. If we daily obey the teaching of the anointing within us, then we abide in Christ, and if we abide in Christ, then every spiritual blessing in the heavenlies has been given to us. So first of all we need to seek for heavenly blessing, spiritual blessing, and not just earthly blessing.

How can we really be blessed with spiritual blessings? We need to be in the heavenlies in Christ Jesus. And if we are there, then all these will be ours because it is the delight of God to bless.

## WHAT ARE THE SPIRITUAL BLESSINGS?

Let's look a little bit at the spiritual blessings He has blessed us with. Ephesians 1:3-14 gives us a bird's eye view of the spiritual blessings that God has blessed us with. It is not exhaustive; it is illustrative. What are these spiritual blessings? When you read that section, probably you will find it is too complicated because when Paul wrote it, his heart was so full, he really was not able to put everything on paper. So out of the fulness of his heart he tried to pile all these things together, one after another, and grammatically he did not mind. But when we read it, it is a little bit difficult. Recently, I was reading it again and as I read it I thought maybe we could divide them into three parts. The first part is the glory of His grace. The second part is the riches of His grace. The third part is the praise of His glory. Maybe dividing into these parts will be a help to us.

## THE GLORY OF HIS GRACE

From Ephesians 1:4-6 we may say it is the glory of His grace. When you come to spiritual blessing, remember it is a matter of grace. It is all grace. Grace means that God provides, God gives to us freely. All we do is receive it by faith with thankfulness. You will find you have done nothing in all these things. It is all His doing. It is His love. It is grace, pure grace. And it said, "The glory of His grace." Whenever you find the word *glory*, you know it has something to do with the purpose of God, the will of God. God is glory; therefore whatever He plans, and whatever He gives of His grace must fit with His glory. What He prepares is for His glory. It is not just for our benefit, but it is for His glory. So His grace is so glorious. Now in what sense is His grace glorious?

## GOD HAS CHOSEN US

"According as he has chosen us in him before the world's foundation." Now did you have anything to do with that? Before the world's foundation, where were you? We are nowhere; and yet before the world's foundation, God has chosen us in Christ Jesus. He chose us not because of us; He chose us because of His Son. Some people may have problems with God's choice or divine election. But I thank God for that because it gives me the firmest assurance. How can I be sure? If I look at myself I cannot be sure for a second. Can you be sure of yourself? What will you be the next moment? Where will you be? We are not sure; but if God has chosen you before the world's foundation nothing can change it. He chose you not because of you; you were not there. You have not spent a day on earth. You have not done anything yet, not even in your mother's womb, and yet God has already chosen you in Christ Jesus. What assurance that gives us! And what love is behind it! He has chosen you before the foundation of the world. Your salvation is not an accident. Are you sure of that? You are on solid ground, on the Rock of Ages.

Then it says, "He has chosen you." For what? "that we should be holy and blameless before Him in love". People today are troubled with this matter of divine election. They say, "Well, I don't know if God has chosen me to be saved." Or they may say, "God has chosen me to be condemned." The Bible does not teach this. When God chose you, it is more than a matter of being saved out of hell into heaven. We think being saved out of hell into heaven is great, that nothing can be greater than that; but to God that is nothing. He has chosen you before the world's foundation. For what? So that He may fill the heaven with people? No; if He really filled the heaven with people like us today, it would become hell. He has chosen us before the world's foundation *that we may be holy.* Our God is holy and because He is holy He wants us to be holy like Him. Holy simply means "separated unto God." We are completely separated from ourselves, from what we are, and completely devoted to Him and what He is. Holy is to be like God. That is godliness, to be like God and to be transformed and conformed to the image of His beloved Son. This is what we are chosen for. You are chosen to be like God's beloved Son, that He may be the first-born among many brethren, leading them into glory. That is what we are chosen with—holy and without blemish, blameless in love. Love covers a multitude of sins.

How can we be without blemish? We are full of spots and wrinkles, but His love will wash us clean that we may be holy and blameless before Him in love. Now that is spiritual blessing.

## GOD HAS MARKED US OUT

Then it says, "Having marked us out beforehand for sonship through Jesus Christ to himself, according to the good pleasure of his will, to the praise of the glory of his grace." He has marked us out. That speaks of what He wants us to be. He has marked us out for sonship, the placing of sons. When we are saved, we are children; we are babes in Christ. But God wants us to grow into maturity, into the fulness of the measure of the stature of Christ. And after we have grown into maturity, He will place us as sons together with His only begotten Son to receive, to be heirs and co-heirs of all things. Now this is what God has chosen us and predestined us to be. So here you find the glory of His grace. It is all His grace. His grace will do the work if only you will allow His grace to work in you. Our problem is we stand against the grace of God. If we allow His grace to work in our lives, He will accomplish it so that God may be glorified. Now that is the glory of His grace.

## THE RICHES OF HIS GRACE

"The riches of His grace." His grace is so rich. The Bible tells us of the unsearchable riches of Christ and these unsearchable riches of Christ are grace to us. So that grace is rich. A few examples are given and one is that He has taken us into favor in the Beloved. Our Lord Jesus is God's favorite and in Christ Jesus, God has taken us into favor. In other words, we become God's favorites in Christ Jesus. Now to be favored by God is something. Being favored by man is nothing, but how we seek to be favored by man. Thank God, by the riches of His grace He has brought us into favor. Every one of us becomes God's favorite. That is the reason why we always feel that God favors us personally so much, as if in the whole world He is just for us. Why? It is because He loves us.

And it says, "We have redemption through His blood." We are redeemed. We were slaves; we were under the curse of the law; we were under bondage. Our future was nothing, eternal death, and yet our Lord Jesus paid a tremendous price for us, even His own blood. He bought us with His own blood. He redeemed us out of the curse of the law, out of the power of darkness and translated us into the kingdom of His love. We can never forget that—forgiveness of our sins. Though our sins are as red as scarlet, they shall be whiter than snow. That is the riches of His grace.

## THE PRAISE OF HIS GLORY

"The praise of his glory." Glory is always connected with God Himself, with His purpose, with His will. So according to His will, what is His eternal purpose? What has He purposed in Himself, even in eternity past? What is it that He has counseled, planned to accomplish in eternity to come? What is it? It is to head up all things in Christ. In God's heart there is only one Person, His beloved Son Christ Jesus. And because of God's love to His own Son, He wants to sum up, to gather up, to head up all things in Christ, things in the heavens, things on the earth; nothing excepted. Everything is to speak of Christ. Everything is to glorify Christ. Everything is to manifest Christ. Today, we have not seen everything under His feet, but we do see Jesus, made a little inferior than the angels for the suffering of death, crowned with glory and honor. So we know that the day is coming, and God is working towards it, to sum up all things in Christ. In other words, whether things in the heavens or things on the earth, when you look at them, you see the glory of Jesus Christ. And thank God, in that plan He has included us. He has joined us to His beloved Son. We are the ones who have pre-trusted in Christ. He has not only given us an inheritance in Christ Jesus, Christ is our inheritance, but He has also made us His inheritance. And it is all through the sealing of the Holy Spirit, the pledge of the Holy Spirit, the working of the Holy Spirit. It is all related to the purpose of God and it is all unto the praise of His glory, that He may be praised.

So what are the spiritual blessings? To put it into one word: Christ. He is the spiritual blessing. Every blessing that God can bless you with is in Him and out of Him. And when you really enter into these blessings, what do you discover? You discover that it is Christ, that He may be all and in all to the glory of God.

Let us pray:

*Dear heavenly Father, we do rejoice in Thy presence, seeing what Thou hast done in Thy beloved Son, our Lord Jesus Christ. Thou hast put all things in Him and Thou hast put us in Him. Dear Lord, we pray that our hearts may be so occupied with Thyself that we may enjoy all these spiritual blessings that Thou hast promised, and in enjoying them, see that it is Christ Himself whom we enjoy. We pray that this may be real and increasingly real to every one of us, to the praise of Your glory. In the name of our Lord Jesus. Amen.*

# THE BLESSED OF THE LORD

*Ephesians 1:3—Blessed be the God and Father of our Lord Jesus Christ, who has blessed us with every spiritual blessing in the heavenlies in Christ.*

*Psalm 1:1-6—Blessed is the man that walketh not in the counsel of the wicked, and standeth not in the way of sinners, and sitteth not in the seat of scorners; but his delight is in Jehovah's law, and in his law doth he meditate day and night. And he is as a tree planted by brooks of water, which giveth its fruit in its season, and whose leaf fadeth not; and all that he doeth prospereth. The wicked are not so; but are as the chaff which the wind driveth away. Therefore the wicked shall not stand in the judgment, nor sinners in the assembly of the righteous. For Jehovah knoweth the way of the righteous, but the way of the wicked shall perish.*

*Matthew 5:1-12—But seeing the crowds, he went up into the mountain, and having sat down, his disciples came to him; and, having opened his mouth, he taught them, saying, Blessed are the poor in spirit, for theirs is the kingdom of the heavens. Blessed they that mourn, for they shall be comforted. Blessed the meek, for they shall inherit the earth. Blessed they who hunger and thirst after righteousness, for they shall be filled. Blessed the merciful, for they shall find mercy. Blessed the pure in heart, for they shall see God. Blessed the peace-makers, for they shall be called sons of God. Blessed they who are persecuted on account of righteousness, for theirs is the kingdom of the heavens. Blessed are ye when they may reproach and persecute you, and say every wicked thing against you, lying, for my sake. Rejoice and exult, for your reward is great in the heavens; for thus have they persecuted the prophets who were before you.*

Shall we pray:

*Dear Lord, our hearts are full. We are most grateful to Thee. Thou who art the Son of God, yet Thou emptied Thyself and took up the form of a slave, the fashion of a man, and Thou being man was obedient unto death, even the death of the cross. And it is all for our sake. We thank Thee. Thou art now exalted on high at the right hand of the Father, waiting for all Thy enemies to be Thy footstool. Thou art worthy. Lord, as we continue in that worshiping spirit, we look to Thee to speak to our hearts. Bless us that we may bless Thee. We commit this time into Thy hands. Deliver us from self-consciousness, Lord, that we may be conscious only of Thy presence. Speak, Lord, Thy servant heareth. In Thy precious name. Amen.*

"Blessed be the God and Father of our Lord Jesus who has blessed us with every spiritual blessing in the heavenlies in Christ Jesus." When the apostle Paul began this letter, his heart was so full that he began with "Blessed be the God and Father of our Lord Jesus Christ." We know that our God is the God of blessing. He loves to bless because He is love, but when we are blessed, do we bless Him because of the blessings He has blessed us with? When we are blessed, do we just take His blessings as ours and enjoy them? If we do, the result is that our hearts will grow fat, and we will soon forget Him and rebel against Him. This was proven in the history of the children of Israel, and we are no different from them.

When we are blessed, if we just take the blessings to ourselves, and let them end with us, the end result will be curse and not blessing. When God blesses us, it is that we may bless Him with the blessing that He has blessed us with. It should not just end in ourselves. If we receive His blessing and we give the blessing back to Him, and bless Him for His blessing, then these blessings will become real blessings in our lives. Everything comes from God and everything returns to God. He is the beginning and He is the end. So when we are blessed, remember it is for Him. It is that we may have something to bless Him with.

"Blessed be the God and Father of our Lord Jesus Christ." When He blesses us, He blesses us as the God and Father of our Lord Jesus Christ. We cannot imagine how God is the God of our Lord Jesus. We cannot imagine how the Father is the Father of our Lord Jesus. Yet, thank God, His Father is our Father and His God is our God. And today, it is in that relationship that God has blessed us with every spiritual blessing.

He has blessed us because He has blessed His Son. He has put every blessing that He can bless with in His beloved Son, and through His beloved Son, He has blessed us with every spiritual blessing. We have mentioned again and again that the real blessing, the blessing that will last forever, is not physical, it is not material, because physical things are temporal and they soon pass away. But spiritual blessing is eternal and God in Christ Jesus has blessed us with every spiritual blessing that we can think of. Why? It is because all the fulness of the Godhead dwells in Christ bodily. Outside of Christ God has no blessing to bless with. Every blessing is in Christ and in Christ He has blessed us with every spiritual blessing. We do not need to go outside of Christ and try to find blessing. As a matter of fact, a blessing that is not in Christ, or even to say a blessing that is not Christ Himself, is not blessing at all.

Sometimes we feel that we are blessed. The world thinks that if we have this, if we have that, then we are blessed, but if what we consider as blessing is not in Christ, is not out of Christ, is not Christ Himself, remember it is not a blessing; it is a curse. I think experience will tell us that. Anything that is not of Christ, anything that is not Christ Himself eventually will prove to not be a blessing. The real blessing is that God blesses us with Christ. When we are blessed with Christ and when every spiritual blessing is just a phase of Christ, an expanse of Christ, then that blessing is everlasting and it is a real blessing. So God has blessed us with every spiritual blessing in the heavenlies.

We have mentioned already that there is a heavenly realm and it is in that heavenly realm that we are blessed with every spiritual blessing. And it is in Christ Jesus. I do not know how to share my heart. I do not have the words for it. The only word I can say is this: What is blessing? The blessing that comes from God is just Christ. That's it! Now if we can only see this, we will be delivered from all kinds of problems and troubles. We will be delivered from all illusions and misconceptions. Just remember that the blessing God has blessed us with is not only *in*

Christ but actually it *is* Christ. When a blessing becomes a Person, you receive the right blessing. If a blessing is just a thing, you may lose it; it may change its nature. But if the blessing is Christ, a Person you come to receive, you come to know, you come to experience, a living Person, then that blessing is everlasting, and this is what God wants to bless us with.

Now we would like to go a step further from blessing to the blessed, from gift to the gifted. In other words, God has blessed us with every spiritual blessing and now in turn we will become the blessed of the Lord.

## WHO ARE THE BLESSED OF THE LORD?

In the Old Testament, when Abraham rescued his nephew Lot and defeated the four kings, Melchisedec, the high priest of God, met him. In Genesis 14 we are told: "Blessed be Abraham of the Most High God, possessor of heaven and earth." Abraham is the blessed one. He was blessed by God. When the God of glory appeared to him in Ur of Chaldea and called him to leave his native country, his kindred, his own family, and go to where God was calling him, he obeyed by faith. Because of this he was blessed. Even in the promised land, he lived there as a stranger and a sojourner. It is this obedience of faith that made him the blessed one, and when he was blessed by God with Isaac, he offered Isaac back to God as the sacrifice of faith. And because of his obedience of faith, his walk of faith, and his sacrifice of faith, Abraham became the blessed one of God. Not only was he blessed by God, but he became a blessing.

In the New Testament, we think of Mary, the mother of our Lord Jesus. In Luke 1, when the angel Gabriel appeared to her, he said, "Hail, thou favored one. The Lord is with you and you are blessed among women." We call Mary the blessed. Why? Because when God called her and wanted to use her, in spite of the fact that she would be misunderstood, she would be rejected, and she would even be stoned to death, yet she said, "Do unto thy handmaiden according to what Thou hast said." That is the abandonment of love. Because of the abandonment of love, she was the blessed one.

How can we be the blessed of the Lord? Who are the blessed? In what position will we be the blessed of the Lord? Now we would like to use two portions of Scripture. One is in the Old Testament; the other is in the New Testament. In the Old Testament we would like to use Psalms. We know that Psalms is a collection of the experiences of those who knew the Lord. They passed through all kinds of circumstances—sometimes prosperity, sometimes adversity, sometimes joy, sometimes sorrow, sometimes life abundant, sometimes the gate of death. The psalmists passed through all kinds of experiences in this world. They experienced every kind of experience you can think of and when they went through all these experiences, they discovered God Himself. They found God to be their blessing, and out of their experiences they wrote these Psalms. So Psalms is a collection; it is not a book of doctrine, but it is a book of experience. And out of experience they learned spiritual blessing, the true blessing of the Lord.

Of course, the first Psalm is an introduction to the one hundred and fifty Psalms. It is the preface. It begins with, "Blessed." Who are the blessed?

Whenever I read this Psalm, I remember a true story. In China we had a fellow worker named Phillip Luan. (The older ones in our midst may still remember.) When he was young, he was sent by his father to Russia to study, where he graduated. In his youth, he even participated in the Russian Revolution. He was from Manchuria, and when he came back and arrived at the railway station in Manchuria, he saw a red cap (that is a coolie) helping people with luggage. He knew that man because he had been a merchant in Russia. So he asked that man what had happened to him. He said, "In Russia I began to be an opium smoker and I lost everything." (This brother himself was an opium smoker and he told us that in Russia they encouraged the Chinese to smoke opium.) Upon hearing that, immediately he felt he had to quit smoking opium. Instead of going home, he went to a hotel; he shut himself into that hotel for three days and three nights. He told us that he was rolling on the floor as the desire for opium came, but he determined he would rather die than smoke opium. In three days, he quit opium. He went home, but he had nothing to do. He came from a very rich family. His brother opened a gold store, and when the Japanese came, they took their land and built an airport.

So he was just staying with his brother, having nothing to do. He did not really know what Christianity was, but he was very anti-Christian. He was just like Saul of Tarsus. In that city there was only one church, but do you know what he did? He employed a group of children to go into that church and when the people stood and sang, they threw sand into their mouths. When they stood and prayed, they moved the chairs away. He did that until that church was closed. He told us that he went from house to house preaching against Christianity. He did not know what Christianity really was because of his education in Russia.

One day, he was in his brother's store with nothing to do. It was raining, so he tried to find something to read. Strangely, he found a book under the table. (It was a hymnbook. I do not know how it came into that house.) He opened that hymnbook and read these words: "Blessed is the man that walketh not in the counsel of the wicked and standeth not in the way of sinners and sitteth not in the seat of scorners." After he read this, he said, "That makes sense."

He could not sleep that night. The next morning he rose up and went to that church building. Of course, it was closed, but he pushed the door and it opened. He went straight to the pulpit. He saw a big book on the table, and when he opened that book, and it was Psalm 1. It was the same words he had read in the hymnbook, and he took the book home. The first time he stole, he stole a Bible. He started to read it and it began to touch his heart.

But he became the leader of the second revolution in Manchuria. In order to promote revolution, there were certain things he had to do. He needed a place where he could make propaganda, and he said the best place was the Y. M. C. A. So he used the Y. M. C. A. as the outlet for propaganda; but in revolution you need money. How could he get money? The best way to get money was to open a cigarette factory. So he opened a cigarette factory and began to produce cigarettes. But all the foreign cigarette companies tried to resist him. All the stores that sold cigarettes were given cigarettes by the foreign cigarette companies and they did not need to pay in advance. They gave them time to pay later. The stores all resisted buying his cigarettes, but he was very clever. He employed a number of people sitting in the rickshaws. (In the old days they had rickshaws.) They would visit all the stores that sold cigarettes, and when they came down from the rickshaw and asked for cigarettes, they would take out this man's package and tell them they wanted this cigarette because it was the best. The stores tried to sell them the other one. "No," they said, "all these others are of no use. If you do not have this one, we won't have any."

These people would go all around the city saying the same thing, and these places said this cigarette has lots of demand. So they began to order his cigarettes, but then he said, "My cigarette is the best; you have to pay cash." So they all paid cash and then he discharged all these people. Now the stores had all these cigarettes, but nobody wanted them. So they began to push the cigarettes for him and advertise them. They became very successful and he had all the money he needed for a revolution. But of course, being the leader of the second revolution, the Japanese wanted to catch him and arrest him, and the warlords wanted to arrest him, so he fled for his life. He told me lots of stories about how he escaped all these arrests. I will give you just one.

He had the names of all the revolutionists in his home. He thought that if the Japanese got hold of those names many people would be arrested and killed. What should he do? He could not go home, so he disguised himself. That night he went back to his home. In Manchuria it is very cold; you cover yourself so that nothing but your two eyes can be seen. When he got to his home, it was dark and the door was closed. He pushed the door and it opened. People were waiting and immediately he was caught. When he was caught, he said, "Sorry, I am just a tailor. This family ordered lots of clothes. I made them, but they have not given me the money." He showed them all the accounts, and then he said, "Sorry, I have to go to the toilet." So he went to the toilet and all the things were hidden there. He pushed it and they were flushed out. That was this brother.

When he was fleeing for his life, one morning, when he was in a strange city, he said the Spirit of God convicted him. All his sins came back to him and he was in the sitting room kneeling there, praying, and his tears wet the carpet. While he was praying the word of God came to him, one after another, comforting him, assuring him, and he was wonderfully saved. And it all began with Psalm 1.

Later on, he closed his factory and went to Shanghai to study the Bible. While he was studying in the Bible institute, he was so anxious to serve the Lord, he rented a place in old Shanghai and employed a preacher to preach for him first, but on weekdays he would come and help. Now that was that brother.

He brought lots of money to Shanghai and put it in the bank, but the Lord dealt with him very severely. The bank went bankrupt. He had tuberculosis, but wonderfully, the Lord raised him up, and the Lord used him mightily in China. It all came from this Psalm 1. So every time I read Psalm 1, I just cannot forget that. "Blessed is the man that walketh not in the counsel of the wicked, and standeth not in the way of sinners, and sitteth not in the seat of scorners."

## WALK NOT IN THE COUNSEL OF THE WICKED

Who is the blessed man? According to the Old Testament, the blessed man is a man who walks not in the counsel of the wicked. Why? It is because in the Old Testament time the emphasis is more on outward conduct. Under the law it is the outward behavior, the outward conduct that matters most. So, who is the man that is the blessed of God? He is the man who walks not in the counsel of the wicked.

You know, the whole world lies under the wicked one. So far as God is concerned, every one in the world is wicked. Among the wicked there may be some who are less wicked, some who are more wicked, but all human beings are wicked because we all lie under the wicked one. And the wicked usually have counsel; they like to have suggestions, plans, projects. All these are wicked because they all lead us away from God. "Walk not in the counsel of the wicked."

## STAND NOT IN THE WAY OF SINNERS

"Stand not in the way of sinners." Everybody in this world is a sinner, less sin or more sin, but sinners. And the sinner has a way. It is the way of the sinners and we are all walking in that way. In Ephesians 2, you will find that we are all dead in sins and transgressions. We all follow the world and its fashion, not knowing that actually we are under the evil spirit. We are the children of wrath. There is a way that we consider as right, but it ends in destruction. Now the blessed one will not walk in the way of the sinners.

## SIT NOT IN THE SEAT OF THE SCORNERS

"Sit not in the seat of the scorners." You find there is a progression there—the wicked, the sinner, the scorners. Not only do they rebel against God, they begin to ridicule God, become scorners, and they sit down. You walk, you stand, and you sit. Those who are blessed of the Lord in their daily life, in their conduct, do not walk in the counsel of the wicked, nor stand in the way of sinners, nor sit in the seat of scorners. Negatively, this is what it is.

## THE BLESSED ARE THOSE WHO LOVE GOD'S WORD

In Psalm 1, verse 2, you have the positive, and the positive actually is the reason why they do not walk and stand and sit. "But his delight is in Jehovah's law and in his law does he meditate day and night." A man that is blessed of the Lord is a person who delights in the law of God, the word of God, and he meditates upon it day and night. The word of God cleanses us. If we love the word of God and if we meditate upon it, that will keep us from walking in the counsel of the wicked, from standing in the way of sinners, and from sitting in the seat of scorners.

Even today, we are to delight in the word of God and meditate upon it day and night. The thing that is very missing today is that we do not meditate on the word of God. Modern life is rushing—just rushing. We do not have the time to really think, rethink, meditate, consider, and because of this our life is very shallow. We need to meditate on the word of God in order that our

48

spiritual life may grow deep. And that will keep us from all these wickednesses, sins, and scornings.

Such a man is like a tree planted by brooks of water. In other words, they are connected with the source of life, and because they are connected with the source of life, therefore they will not fail to produce fruit. And fruit here means something that comes from within; it is the riches of the life within that is expressed in fruits. Those who really love the word of God and meditate on the word of God will have fruit, the fruit of the Spirit. And they will have leaves. Their leaves will not fade, and leaves simply means our outward conduct. Outwardly, there will be good behavior that will glorify God. And their undertakings will be prospered by God. In the Old Testament, of course we know that their blessing was mainly earthly, even though some with faith could go further into spiritual blessing. These are the blessed in the Old Testament time.

## THE LIFE OF THE WICKED

On the contrary, what happened to the wicked? "The wicked are not so; but are as the chaff which the wind driveth away." There is no life in chaff. It cannot be eaten and when the wind blows, it blows away; it disappears. That is the life of the wicked. The life of the blessed is like trees; there is root. But the life of the wicked is like chaff—no root. It is just empty, transient, and it just blows away. And because God is the judge, eventually the wicked will be judged, and they will not stand in the assembly of the righteous because God knows our way. Now this is in the Old Testament time.

Sometimes you find in this world there are the wicked, but they seem to prosper. And there are the righteous that seem to suffer. This is a question that has been asked throughout the centuries. If you read Psalm 73 this righteous one is asking this question: "Why do the wicked prosper and the righteous suffer?" Sometimes it may appear that way. He said, "Until I go into the sanctuary, then I know. God is the judge and the prosperity of the wicked is just for a time. But the righteous will inherit eternally." So this is what we find in the Old Testament. In the Old Testament time, of course, the blessed is more concerned with outward behavior, but thank God, today, in Christ Jesus, we are redeemed. We become the heavenly and the spiritual people of God.

## THE BEATITUDES

Who are the blessed in the New Testament time? In Matthew 5, our Lord Jesus went to the mountain. Great crowds came to Him, so He left the crowd and climbed the mountain, and His disciples came to Him. So He opened His mouth and taught His disciples. The Sermon on the Mount begins with *blessed*. Who are the truly blessed?

## BLESSED ARE THE POOR IN SPIRIT

"Blessed are the poor in spirit for theirs is the kingdom of the heavens." In Luke 6:20-26 you find a little variation there:

*And he (our Lord), lifting up his eyes upon his disciples, said, Blessed are ye poor, for yours is the kingdom of God. Blessed ye that hunger now, for ye shall be filled. Blessed ye that weep now, for ye shall laugh. Blessed are ye when men shall hate you, and when they shall separate you from them, and shall reproach you, and cast out your name as wicked, for the Son of man's sake: rejoice in that day and leap for joy, for behold, your reward is great in the heaven, for after this manner did their fathers act toward the prophets. But woe to you rich, for ye have received your consolation. Woe to you that are filled, for ye shall hunger. Woe to you who laugh now, for ye shall mourn and weep. Woe, when all men speak well of you, for after this manner did their fathers to the false prophets.*

You find there is a slight difference between these two passages. In Matthew our Lord spoke to His disciples telling them who are the blessed. So it is instruction. But in Luke you find our Lord lifted up His eyes and looked at His disciples. In other words, these disciples had been taught, and being taught, the Lord said, "Blessed ye the poor." So in Luke it is more simple. It does not say, "Blessed are the poor in spirit." Of course, in reality it is; but it says, "Blessed ye the poor, for yours is the kingdom of God." The Lord is not referring to these disciples as the physically, materially poor. While these disciples were not rich in any sense, John and James, even though they were fishermen, had a  father who had hired hands and boats, so they were not really poor. When the Lord looked at the disciples, the Lord said, "Blessed ye, the poor." So the poor there does not refer to the materially, physically, naturally poor. The "poor" there refers to them becoming the disciples of the Lord and therefore they become the poor.

You remember in II Corinthians 8 it says our Lord being rich, yet He became poor for our sake. In Philippians 2, we find that He is equal with God and that is not something to be grasped at because He is God; He is the Son of God. The Son and the Father are one. And yet, He emptied Himself. You cannot think of anyone richer than our Lord. Who can be richer than God? The whole world belongs to Him. Everything is His. Our Lord is the richest in the whole universe. He has the universe, but He emptied Himself. He became poor for our sakes that we may be enriched in Him.

So who are the disciples? Who are the learners, the followers of our Lord Jesus? You remember when our Lord Jesus called His disciples: "Come after Me." They left everything and followed Him. That made them poor. It is voluntary poverty. For the sake of the Lord they left everything behind and followed the Lord and the Lord said, "Blessed ye, the poor, for yours is the kingdom of God."

What is a disciple? Disciple simply means learner. You learn from your master. Who is the master? When you look at the Sermon on the Mount, at the Beatitudes, it is actually a description of the character of our Lord Jesus. That is what He is. He is the most blessed one because He is the poor in spirit. He is the one who mourns. He is the meek, He is the one who thirsts and hungers after righteousness. He is the merciful. He is the pure in heart. He is the peacemaker. He is the persecuted for righteousness' sake. It is a description of the character of our Lord Jesus when He was on earth. He is the Master, the teacher, and He is calling us to be His disciples. Today, we tend to divide believers and disciples. We think we can be believers and not be disciples. But in the early days, there was no separation. If you believed in Him, then you followed Him. If you received Him as your Savior, then you surrendered to Him as your Master, as your Lord.

I think probably many brothers and sisters know the story of Watchman Nee when he was saved. He knew the doctrines, the gospel, and when he went to hear Miss Dora Yu, on the first night when he listened he knew it was all true. The gospel is true. Jesus Christ is true. His salvation is real and he knew that he should believe, but he did not that night. He struggled for a number of nights. The problem was that he knew that if he received Jesus as his Savior then he must surrender to Jesus as his Lord. He could not do that. As a young man he had his own plans. And he would be successful from the human standpoint. It was hard for him to give up. He struggled and struggled, until one day when he was praying, he saw the blackness of his sins and the redness of the blood of the Lord. He was moved by the love of Christ and he capitulated. He believed in Jesus as his Savior, and at the same time he accepted Jesus as his Lord and Master.

When we receive Jesus as our Savior, do we surrender our life to Him as our Lord and Master? This is discipleship. Do we give ourselves away, leave everything, and follow Him? In other words, in becoming disciples we become poor voluntarily, leave everything behind and just follow Him. He is our riches, our wealth, our all. "Blessed ye, the poor."

So when you come to Matthew, it explains what that *poor* means. He said, "Blessed are the poor in spirit." Before we believe in the Lord Jesus, we are very rich in ourselves. We think highly of ourselves. We are capable; we have lots of ability and talents. We can do this; we can do that. We can even save ourselves, and we try. But thank God, He bankrupts us. We come to a point where we find that we can do nothing. We cannot save ourselves. Our righteousnesses are as filthy rags. They will not meet the demands of the righteous God. We are reduced to poverty, spiritual poverty, and it is then that we receive the Lord as our Savior. Blessed are the poor in spirit.

It does not mean that we have a poor spirit. You know, some people have a poor spirit. That is different from poor in spirit. If you are a poor-spirited person, there is no blessing there. But if you are poor in spirit, you are reduced to poverty, reduced to nothing, you begin to have that spirit of humility, self-effacement. How can you be reduced to that—to nothing? Naturally, we all think highly of ourselves. We think we are somebody, we are something, we have something, but when we see the glory of God, when we see the face of the Lord Jesus, when we see His riches, when we see His beauty, that turns our beauty into corruption.

You remember the story of Daniel. When he was just in his teens, he was taken as a hostage to a foreign country. He was given the best opportunity; and yet how he kept himself pure for the Lord. He would not defile himself with the king's food and wine. He was such a young man, and God blessed him with wisdom, understanding, and discernment. Yet in his old age, when he saw the beauty of the Lord, the glory of the Lord, he said, "My beauty was turned into corruption."

If you see the Lord, if you follow Him—you cannot see Him if you do not follow Him—if you follow Him and you see Him, what will happen? It will bring you into spiritual poorness. He will reduce you to being poor in spirit. The spirit of Christ is the spirit of the Lamb. It is a spirit of humility and that spirit will characterize your spirit and that is the way to blessing.

Do you know why we are not being blessed as we should? So far as God is concerned, He has blessed us with every spiritual blessing in the heavenlies in Christ. Why is it we do not receive the blessing as we should? It is because we are too full, we are too rich in ourselves. We are just like the Laodicean Church: "I am rich, I do not lack anything. I have everything, I have knowledge, I have understanding, I have everything." That kind of spirit blocks the way to blessing.

So dear brothers and sisters, to begin with, if we want to be the blessed of the Lord, where should we be? We have to be in the low place—not physically but spiritually—poor in spirit. We acknowledge, we confess we are nothing, that within us there is nothing. But as a matter of fact, the more that you know you are nothing, actually the more you have something. It is the poor in spirit who are rich spiritually because they will be filled. If we empty ourselves, then He will fill us.

"Theirs is the kingdom of the heavens." We do not need to wait until the future to get into the kingdom of the heavens. Today, among God's people, many do not even know there is the kingdom. They think that there is today and eternity, this age and eternity. They do not even know there is the age to come, the kingdom. But those who are poor in spirit are the blessed because even today they are already in the kingdom of the heavens because that is the very atmosphere of the kingdom of the heavens. In the kingdom of the heavens there is no quarreling of who is the greatest. In the kingdom of the heavens he who is the smallest is the greatest. The poor in spirit live even today in the kingdom of the heavens. And only those who today live in the kingdom of the heavens will be qualified to reign with Christ in the kingdom to come. So the blessed of the Lord in the New Testament time begins with the spirit of humility. So may the Lord keep us in that spirit.

As you look into church history, whether referring to a group or to individuals, you will find the reason why those who are blessed of the Lord begin to fall is because they lack the spirit of humility. If you look at church history, you would think it is as if the blessing of the Lord cannot maintain more than twenty or thirty years. After thirty years there is a declension, and it is repeated again and again; but is it the will of God? Certainly not! The reason why you find declension after twenty or thirty years of being blessed is always because you become full in yourself. You are proud of the blessing of God. You have the blessing but you lose the Blessor; you lose sight of Christ. You only see the blessing He blessed you with. You separate blessings from the Blessor and that is the declension. But it should not be. If only by the grace of God you are kept in a humble spirit, then you will find you are the blessed. The blessing will continue and you will be found even today, to be living in the kingdom of the heavens.

## BLESSED ARE THEY THAT MOURN

"Blessed they that mourn, for they shall be comforted." Why is it that those who mourn today are blessed? It is because they grieve according to God. If you grieve according to the world, there is no blessing there, but if you grieve according to God, then it will lead to repentance unto salvation. So blessed are those who mourn for they shall be comforted.

## BLESSED ARE THE MEEK

"Blessed the meek, for they shall inherit the earth." Who are the meek? In Matthew 11:29 our Lord Jesus said, "Take My yoke upon you and learn of Me, for I am meek and lowly of heart and you shall find rest in your soul." So our Lord Jesus is the meek One. If we take His yoke upon us, we have to be yoked with Christ. We cannot learn meekness if we are not yoked with Him. He is on one side of the yoke; He is the meek One. We are the haughty one, and we are on the other side of the yoke. When we are pulling the plow, we find that He, the meek one is stronger than the haughty one, and He will pull us in His direction. By that we begin to learn meekness. If you are not yoked with Christ, you will never learn meekness because naturally we are haughty. We have to be yoked with Christ; that is discipleship. We learn from Christ. Then there will be meekness in us.

The Bible says that Moses is the meekest of all men. Now certainly that is not our impression. When the artist draws Moses, what kind of face does he have? What are the features? It is so masculine. But in Numbers 12, the Bible says Moses is the meekest of all people. Certainly he is not weak, but where is meekness? What is meekness? Meekness means he is soft, tender to the will of God. Whatever is the will of God, he will do it. When he was commanded to build the tabernacle, and was given the pattern on the mount, even to the minutest detail, he did not deviate a bit. even though he had been trained in Egypt, a great architect.. He followed the directions. He was meek toward the will of God. That is meekness.

Are we meek? It does not mean you are weak. We think of meek as being like jelly—no backbone, no principle. No, meek is not weak. Meek simply means that before God, before His will, you are so meek you will do everything that He orders you. That is meekness. And if you are meek, the world will say you will get nothing, but God will give you the land.

## Blessed Are Those Who Hunger and Thirst After Righteousness

"Blessed they who hunger and thirst after righteousness, for they shall be filled." Are we hungry and thirsty after righteousness? Of course the righteousness here is not 'Christ our righteousness, period'. You know, we have no righteousness of our own. We are like a prodigal son. When we came back, we were in rags, dirty rags. But when the Father met us, He took off our dirty rags. He put the best robe upon us and the best robe is Christ—Christ our righteousness. God made Christ our righteousness. We are all clothed with Christ and because we are clothed with Christ, we can stand before God without shame, accepted in the Beloved.

The righteousness here is different. It is the righteousness that exceeds the righteousness of the scribes and the Pharisees. The scribes and the Pharisees had a kind of righteousness. It was just an outward appearance, a good appearance. Outwardly, they appeared to be very pious— they kept the letter of the law, even to the minutest degree— but inside it was like a tomb with all these dead bones. Our righteousness must exceed the righteousness of the scribes and Pharisees. Unless we exceed their righteousness we cannot enter into the kingdom of the heavens.

What is that righteousness? "Seek ye first the kingdom of God and His righteousness and all these things shall be added unto you." So the righteousness there is the righteousnesses *of the saints*. You find in Revelation 19 the wife of the Lamb was given a white, shiny, linen garment which is the righteousnesses of the saints. That is the wedding garment.

In Psalm 45 we are told that the queen inside has a garment of wrought gold, and that speaks of Christ our righteousness. Over this golden garment, there is a raiment of embroidery, and that is the wedding garment. The raiment of embroidery means that the Holy Spirit weaves the character of Christ stitch by stitch into our very being. So Christ begins to appear in our life. His character begins to become our character. It is the righteousnesses of the saints, but it is Christ. It is Christ. We need to hunger and thirst after this righteousness, and if we do we will be filled. Thank God for that.

## BLESSED ARE THE MERCIFUL

"Blessed the merciful, for they shall receive mercy." God does not want sacrifice; He wants mercy. He knows our heart. Man judges by appearance but God judges by the heart, and He wants us to be merciful. Our Lord is the merciful One and He wants us to be merciful. We who have received mercy, we should show mercy. You remember that parable of the servant that owed his master so much and was forgiven, but he would not forgive his fellow companion that owed him a little bit. And the Lord said, "Because you are not merciful you will not receive mercy." May the Lord help us.

## BLESSED ARE THE PURE IN HEART

"Blessed the pure in heart for they shall see God." The pure in heart are those who have not only a clean heart but a pure heart, not a double heart, a hardened heart, but an undivided heart towards the Lord. If our heart is undivided towards the Lord, we will see God. The reason why we do not see God in our daily life is because our heart is divided. If it is united, one—love the Lord your God with all your heart—then we will see God in our daily life.

## BLESSED ARE THE PEACEMAKERS

"Blessed the peacemakers, for they shall be called sons of God." Our Lord is the peacemaker, and because He is, when we take up His character, we also become peacemakers. God has given us the ministry of reconciliation, begging the world to be reconciled to God in Christ Jesus.

## BLESSED ARE THEY WHO ARE PERSECUTED FOR MY NAME'S SAKE

"Blessed they who are persecuted for my name's sake, for theirs is the kingdom of the heavens." We do not belong to this world. And because we do not belong, and are not of this world as Christ is not of this world, therefore the world will not understand us. They will not only misunderstand us, they will persecute us. But if we are persecuted for His name's sake, rejoice, for great is your reward in the kingdom of heaven.

So who are the blessed? How can we be in a position of being blessed? Remember the Beatitudes. If we really learn of Him and take up His character in us then there is no limit to the blessing of God. May the Lord help us.

Shall we pray:

*Dear Lord, You are the blessed One, and You want us to be joined to You that we may be blessed. Lord, we do pray that we may learn of You, that Thy character become our character. Lord, all this is for You. We want to bless You with what You have blessed us with. In the name of our Lord Jesus. Amen.*

.

# Other Books Printed By
# Christian Testimony Ministry

| SPEAKER | TITLE |
|---|---|
| DANA CONGDON | MARRIAGE, SINGLENESS, AND THE WILL OF GOD |
| | RECOVERY & RESTORATION |
| | THE HOLY SPIRIT |
| | HEBREWS |
| | |
| A.J. FLACK | TENT OF HIS SPLENDOUR |
| | |
| STEPHEN KAUNG | ACTS |
| | BE YE THEREFORE PERFECT |
| | CALLED OUT UNTO CHRIST |
| | CALLED TO THE FELLOWSHIP OF GOD'S SON |
| | DIVINE LIFE AND ORDER |
| | FOR ME TO LIVE IS CHRIST |
| | GLORIOUS LIBERTY OF THE CHILDREN OF GOD |
| | GOD'S PURPOSE FOR THE FAMILY |
| | I WILL BUILD MY CHURCH |
| | MEDITATIONS ON THE KINGDOM |
| | RECOVERY |
| | SPIRITUAL EXERCISE |
| | SPIRITUAL LIFE (II CORINTHIANS SERIES) |
| | TEACH US TO PRAY |
| | THE CROSS |
| | THE FULNESS OF CHRIST—IN THE BOOK OF REVELATION |
| | THE HEADSHIP OF CHRIST |
| | THE KINGDOM AND THE CHURCH |
| | THE KINGDOM OF GOD |
| | THE LAST CALL TO THE CHURCHES, THE CALL TO OVERCOME |
| | THE LIFE OF OUR LORD JESUS |
| | THE LIFE OF THE CHURCH, THE BODY OF CHRIST |
| | THE LORD'S TABLE |
| | TWO GUIDEPOSTS FOR INHERITING THE KINGDOM |
| | VISION OF CHRIST (REVELATION) |
| | WHO ARE WE? |

WHY DO WE SO GATHER?
WORSHIP

LANCE LAMBERT      CALLED UNTO HIS ETERNAL GLORY
GOD'S ETERNAL PURPOSE
IN THE DAY OF THY POWER
JACOB I HAVE LOVED
LIVING FAITH
LESSONS FROM THE LIFE OF MOSES
LOVE DIVINE
MY HOUSE SHALL BE A HOUSE OF PRAYER
PREPARATION FOR THE COMING OF THE LORD
REIGNING WITH CHRIST
SPIRITUAL CHARACTER
THE GOSPEL OF THE KINGDOM
THE IMPORTANCE OF COVERING
THE LAST DAYS AND GOD'S PRIORITIES
THE PRIZE
THE SUPREMACY OF JESUS CHRIST
THINE IS THE POWER!
THOU ART MINE

T. AUSTIN-SPARKS      THE LORD'S TESTIMONY AND THE WORLD NEED


HARVEY CEDARS CONFERENCE

STEPHEN KAUNG      HEAVENLY VISION
SPIRITUAL RESPONSIBILITY

CONGDON, HILE, KAUNG      SPIRITUAL MINISTRY
SPIRITUAL AUTHORITY
SPIRITUAL HOUSE
SPIRITUAL SUBMISSION

STEPHEN KAUNG      SPIRITUAL KNOWLEDGE
SPIRITUAL POWER
SPIRITUAL REALITY
SPIRITUAL VALUE
SPIRITUAL BLESSING
SPIRITUAL DISCERNMENT

69

SPIRITUAL WARFARE
SPIRITUAL ASCENDANCY
SPIRITUAL MINDEDNESS
SPIRITUAL PERFECTION
SPIRITUAL FULNESS
SPIRITUAL SONSHIP
SPIRITUAL STEWARDSHIP
SPIRITUAL TRAVAIL
SPIRITUAL INHERITANCE
HARVEY CEDARS CONFERENCE:
HILE, KAUNG, LAMBERT
THE KING IS COMING

www.ingramcontent.com/pod-product-compliance
Lightning Source LLC
Chambersburg PA
CBHW060702030426
42337CB00017B/2715